ONLINE COLLEGE
SUCCESS

Prepare, Manage, And Achieve Success
in Online Education

Jim Harger, M.S., M.A

To all my students.

Hopefully, you have learned as much from me as I have from you.

Praise for *Online College Success: Prepare, Manage, and Achieve Success in Online Education*

"Filled with practical, easy-to-follow advice, *Online College Success: Prepare, Manage, and Achieve Success in Online Education* is a must-read book for students taking (or thinking about taking) online courses. The author applies years of online teaching experience to reveal the "hidden" strategies that maximize student success in the online classroom. This book is the ultimate guide for students seeking realistic, doable guidance for navigating the challenges of online learning."

-**Dr. Jean Mandernack**
Executive Director
Center for Innovation in Research and Teaching
Grand Canyon University

"The trend toward online education is growing faster than ever and is broadening beyond the non-traditional student to now include a growing population of traditional online students. That's what makes this book so timely and beneficial. Jim's extensive knowledge and experience in preparing students for this type of program is evident throughout this book. I recommend it for anyone contemplating an online degree or enrolling in an online program."

-**Mike Moroney**
President and Founder of MMC Consulting
Vice President of Enrollment Management
University of Northwestern St. Paul

"Jim Harger captures in a concise, but thorough, way what every non-traditional student needs to be a success in college! Especially helpful was his discussion on the two topics students bring up the most: finances and time management. His solutions for and understanding of the adult student are invaluable. I would recommend this book as required reading for all of our new enrollment counselors."

-**Darris Stauffer**
Regional Enrollment Director

"*Online College Success* is short, easy to read, clearly formatted, and brim full of practical ideas, resources, and personal examples from Jim's extensive teaching career. I found myself nodding 'Yes' to his advice and experiences, and wishing that this resource had been available to me, even as a teacher. Any student who has the desire and self-discipline to read and apply the advice in this book will succeed. No doubt. I can't wait to make it available to my students."

-**Dr. Paul R. Cole**
Affiliate Faculty

"*Online College Success* addresses the apprehensions of rookie online students, and anticipates the issues they will likely encounter in the first weeks of class. In a clear and engaging manner, Jim Harger draws from his experience as an online student, instructor, and administrator to give online students the content and confidence they need to achieve their academic goals."

-**Kirsten Wilson**
Affiliate Faculty

"Whether you are preparing to take your first online course or you've been taking online courses for a while, this book will give you the straightforward advice you need to get organized, achieve your goals, and be successful in the online learning environment. Mr. Harger writes in a friendly, conversational tone which is free from jargon (a welcome relief from other technical resources about technology in education). Throughout each chapter, he shares personal stories and integrates examples from his own experience as both an online teacher and an online student. Mr. Harger's book is a resource both new online students and experienced online students will benefit from."

-Barbi Honeycutt, Ph.D.
FLIP It Consulting & barbihoneycutt.com

"Jim's book is a great introduction to online learning for adult students. He covers the nuts-and-bolts that students are often unaware of, preparing them for a smooth start to their education."

-Dr. Kristen Wall
Director of Institutional Effectiveness

"This book is full of valuable information written in a clear, concise way without excess verbiage. It provides a framework for success for students and should be an encouraging read to those who are nervous about beginning their college journey."

-**Adam Hone**
College Student

TABLE OF CONTENTS

INTRODUCTION

What Makes This Book Different?

I want to commend you! Earning a degree is not easy. It is an investment of time and money. Earning a degree will not only help you achieve your goals, but you will also learn more about yourself and who you are as a person.

If you are reading this book, you are probably considering the option of taking classes online. Like many students, you may feel hesitant or nervous about it. You may think it will be a totally different experience from taking a class in the traditional setting of a classroom. You may have the perception that you will feel isolated and alone.

I understand why you may feel that way. It was not too long ago when I took my first online class. Like you, I had many reservations about it. I remember asking myself, how is this going to work? What do I do if I have a question about an assignment? Will

I miss the experience of sitting in a classroom with my instructor and classmates?

As I began to do the work in my online class, I found that most of my reservations were unfounded. Many of the perceptions I had were not true at all! While the online class experience was different, I was surprised at how similar it was to an in-seat class. I had the same lectures, reading assignments, papers to write, and class discussions as students taking the class on campus. The difference was how I participated and engaged in these activities.

For instance, rather than going to a classroom at a specified time and sitting amongst my classmates, I attended classes through my computer, using the Internet, when it is convenient for me. Instead of sitting in a large room listening to my instructor give a lecture, I watched the same lecture in a video on my computer. The difference was I could watch the lecture at a time that worked best for me. Another big advantage was I could watch it again if I wanted to!

Instead of participating in a discussion with everyone in the same room, I read my classmates' comments on my computer, and then responded in the discussion forum. I loved this because I never felt put on the spot during the discussion. I could think it through before posting it to the discussion. The bottom line is, I began to feel more comfortable in a learning environment and appreciated the flexibility it gave me in completing my class work.

The challenge was sticking with it long enough until I reached a level of comfort and understood how everything worked. The initial phase was a bit awkward, and it took a lot of time to get used to before I felt comfortable and confident in my ability as a student.

The purpose of this book is to help you avoid this awkward phase and get a quick start and establish good habits. I know you want to make the most of your education from the beginning! In addition to helping you prepare for your first class, we will discuss techniques that successful students use in managing their online education, as well as strategies to make the most of the different activities, such as participating in discussions and writing papers.

WHAT EXACTLY IS A NON-TRADITIONAL STUDENT?

Many of you are part of a growing majority of students known as non-traditional students—those students who cannot attend classes on campus in the traditional manner due to their responsibilities with family, work, and other areas of life. Most classes offered on campus are scheduled during the day, which makes it difficult to keep a full-time job. I was a non-traditional student, so I know the challenges you face every day. It's not easy, but it can be done!

Speaking of challenges, as a non-traditional student, unforeseeable obstacles can and will arise and try to throw you off course. Do not let them! With proper preparation, planning, and perseverance, you can manage and overcome these obstacles and challenges.

MY EXPERIENCE

Before we begin, you may want to know a little about me, including what gives me the credibility and expertise to write this book. First, I have over 200 credit hours as a non-traditional student, culminating in two master's degrees, one of which was completed entirely online. Second, I worked in the administration of a university where I managed the day-to-day activities of a center for adult and graduate studies. And third, I have been teaching non-traditional students for ten years. Just in the past five years, I have taught over 150 classes at regionally accredited colleges and universities, most of which were taught online. You can read more about my educational journey in the *About the Author* section at the end of the book.

Suffice it to say, I know what it takes to be a successful online student, both in traditional and non-traditional education. What makes this book different from other books is the fact that I have the perspective of a student, administrator, and instructor. I give you suggestions on how to be a successful student from all three perspectives.

I have full confidence in your ability to meet the academic challenge of an online education. Taking classes online is not easy; it takes self-discipline, self-motivation, and a sizeable dash of organization. With these skills and attitudes, you will find the online format manageable, the content enlightening, and the learning experience rewarding.

You can do this! So, let's get started.

Jim Harger, M.S., M.A.

PREPARE FOR SUCCESS

You have probably heard the saying, "proper preparation prevents poor performance," or some variation of it. Well, it is true. No matter what the task or project, you will have a better outcome if you prepare first.

In this section, we will look at four basic things that you should do to properly prepare before your first class begins: 1) Get the right equipment, 2) become computer literate, 3) purchase your textbooks, and 4) orient yourself to the virtual classroom.

Give ordinary people the right tools,
and they will design and build the most extraordinary things.
~ Neil Gershenfeld ~

COMPUTERS, SOFTWARE, AND ACCESS

Attempting to take online classes without the right equipment can be like trying to cook dinner without pots and pans or repair a motor without tools. You do not need to have the latest and greatest computer or laptop to be a successful student, but you do need one.

COMPUTERS

Occasionally students attempt to take online courses without a computer of their own. Instead, they look to use other people's computers.

You may think you can depend on using a computer that belongs to a friend or family member. This may be a good option, depending on your situation. But what do you do if it is unavailable? You may want to do your homework late in the evening after the kids are in bed. Is your friend going to let you use their computer then?

I have heard of some students using a computer at work. Again, this may work for you, but there may be limitations on that, too. Your boss might not appreciate you doing your homework on company time. And doing it during your lunch limits the time you have to complete your assignments. Also, you will have little to no breaks during the day if you work right through lunch.

Another option is to go to the nearest public library and use the computers there. The trouble with that is there are limits on when you can access the computers. Study hours at the library are limited to when the building is open. Then, you are limited to if, and when, computers are available for use. Often the library sets a one-hour usage limit, as well. If you simply need a computer to submit your work, using a computer at the library is a good option. However, if you must read articles or watch videos and do your homework, then the limited access at the library might not be sufficient for you to meet deadlines.

Any one of these options can work as a short-term option, but in the long term, it will be challenging to keep up. When you have to depend on using someone else's equipment, it practically eliminates the benefit of taking online classes. Instead, you are at the mercy of their schedule. Add to that your obligations and responsibilities to family and work, and you are constricted even more. To maintain the benefit of flexibility, you need your own computer.

MINIMUM REQUIREMENTS FOR A COMPUTER

So, if you do not own a computer, hopefully, I have convinced you that it is a worthwhile investment. This is no reason to panic. Believe it or not, you can get a decent laptop computer for around $300. If you do not believe me, just look up all the options on Amazon. com and see for yourself. Last time we checked, there were over 500 available. I recommend a laptop over a desktop computer primarily because they are portable.

Below is a list of the minimum system requirements that most schools suggest. Keep these in mind as you look at computers, but be sure to check with your institution for specific requirements and recommendations before you purchase a computer.

- Processor: 2.4 GHz minimum for PCs, or Mac equivalent (2.4 GHz dual core or better recommended)

- RAM: 2 GB DDR3 RAM (4 GB or higher recommended)

- Hard disk space: 50 GB (120 GB or higher recommended)

- Operating system: Windows 7 or higher (Windows PC), OS El Capitan (Mac)

- Screen Resolution: 1024x768 or higher

- Webcam: Built-in or external

- Microphone: Built-in or external

- High-speed Internet connection (10 Mbps or higher) for downloading and uploading videos and other media

MOBILE DEVICES

Some students try to complete their assignments on a mobile device such as a smartphone or tablet. Granted, these devices are very advanced, and in many ways, they are a small computer. In addition, more schools are incorporating mobile-friendly applications. Even so, there are limitations to what a user can and cannot do on such a device.

I recently met with a web designer who showed me the difference when users view our website on a mobile device. When a website is viewed on a mobile device, some things get left out for the sake of viewing space. Users may not even realize what is missing until they view the site on a full-size computer screen.

The same goes when viewing reading assignments, videos, and other features of your online class on a mobile device. Some things may be left out for the sake of space.

Another thing to consider is the ergonomics and your physical comfort level working on such a small screen. Many online class assignments involve writing papers and discussion posts. You may find it difficult to write a 1,000-word paper using the keyboard on your phone.

Many of the papers you'll write will require a specific format, such as American Psychological Association (APA) or Modern Language Association (MLA) writing styles. No matter how skilled you may be at typing on a mobile device, you will probably get very frustrated trying to format your paper on one. Trying to adjust margins, paragraph settings, or inserting and formatting the header can be very difficult, if not impossible, on a smartphone or tablet. There are limitations to what you can do on a mobile device.

With that in mind, it is best to use mobile devices as a supplement to your computer or laptop. You can check your email, read posts to threaded discussions, and even write a response to a discussion post on a mobile device. But to access everything and work most effectively, you will want to work on a computer or laptop.

INTERNET

Once you have the appropriate hardware, you need to consider the services and software to complete your basic package. Then you will have a strong supporting bridge to cross the digital divide. As the last item on that list indicated, one service you'll need is access to the

Internet. In the media-rich environment of online classes, dial-up is no longer enough. You need DSL or high-speed Internet service.

Your choice of which Internet browser to use can also make a difference. The two browsers that work best with most learning management systems (LMS) are Google Chrome and Mozilla Firefox. Both these browsers are free and recommended by most schools. Using other browsers may affect your user experience or create access and interactivity issues, which can lead to problems submitting assignments or reading your feedback. It's not worth the risk or the frustration.

SOFTWARE

When it comes to software, you'll need a copy of Microsoft Word, Excel, and PowerPoint. All three of these software packages are a part of the Microsoft Office suite, which you can get with a subscription to Office 365, which is available for both PCs and Macs. Many schools provide student discounts or free subscriptions to Office 365, which gives you the ability to download the complete Office suite onto your computer. Later, you might need additional programs—such as if you are pursuing certain degrees or specialties—but this will get you started and serve you well.

Mac users beware. While Mac does offer similar word processing products such as Pages and Keynote, documents written with these apps are not viewable by PC owners, who include most instructors. You can save them as a PDF document, but many instructors will not accept assignments submitted in this format, either. You can also save your document as a Word document, but sometimes the formatting is a bit different. The best option is to use the Mac version of Microsoft Word, PowerPoint and other apps, which are available with a subscription to Office 365.

One last thing. With a subscription to Office 365, you can also download the suite of apps to your mobile device. Having Word on your smartphone or tablet enables you to write out a short response to a discussion or to make small edits to a document, but there are limitations. It is convenient, though, to have this ability when needed.

CLOUD STORAGE

Another application you will want to have on your computer and mobile device is a service to store and sync your documents to the cloud, such as Dropbox, Google Docs, iCloud, or others. Storing your documents in the cloud gives you the ability to retrieve them from anywhere on any device. Most of these types of services have a free option that should give you plenty of storage space. In addition to storing your documents in the cloud, which serves as a backup if your computer should crash, your documents will be synchronized on all your devices. This is a great feature! If you make any changes to a document on your smartphone or tablet, those changes will be on the document the next time you open it on your computer. It is a great time saver!

Another benefit of cloud storage is you can log in to your cloud storage account using the Internet from any computer, such as the computer at the library. If you ever find yourself somewhere and need to access your documents, just log in to your account and download the document.

All the services are similar and work about the same, so check them out and choose the one that works best for you.

SUMMARY

Here is a summary of what you need to make the most of your education:

- Computer (laptop preferred)

- Good Internet service provider (ISP) (DSL or high-speed)

- Subscription to Office 365 (Word, Excel, and PowerPoint)

- Cloud storage service (such as Dropbox or Google Docs)

Having the right equipment, software programs, and services is like having a super power to get the job done right. With them, you'll be working smarter, not harder.

COMPUTER LITERACY
SKILLS: *LITERALLY REQUIRED*

Tools are only as effective as the person using them. And to be a successful online student, you must have basic computer skills. The good news is, you can learn almost everything you need to know about using a computer, such as using the Internet, email, and other computer functions, through video tutorials. Many schools offer a variety of video tutorials as part of their Student Resources. You may also want to check out GCFLearnFree.org, which offers many free tutorials on how to use different computer programs and applications.

Good computer literacy skills will serve you well not only in college, but also in your workplace. In 2015, eight out of ten middle-level jobs already required basic digital skills. Among those, digitally intensive, middle-skill jobs grew 4.7%, compared to 1.9% for basic-skill positions and offered 18% higher wages. These are jobs that focus on basic everyday software, such as spreadsheets, word processors, billing programs, etc. Taking classes online is digitally intensive, as well. Brush up on the basics and commit to polishing your skills as you progress through your studies. The benefits will pay off in many ways, both in school and in your career.

Basic computer literacy skills provide a foundation for navigating the LMS, which is how your courses are delivered to you over the Internet. The LMS is how you access your reading assignments and videos, engage with your classmates and instructor, and where you submit your assignments for grading. Blackboard, Desire2Learn, and Moodle are common LMS platforms for higher education. A growing number of alternative learning platforms are also available to everyone, such as those found at Teachable.com or Udemy.com.

INTERNET

Since your classes are provided to you through the Internet, you need to know how to navigate it. Most of you probably already know the basics of using the Internet, so I will list only a few things that you should know to make your online experience better.

You should know how to bookmark websites. This is how you save the Internet address of your favorite websites or those that you frequently visit. You will want to bookmark the web address for your school, the LMS website (such as Blackboard), the online access to the university library, and other links. How you do this depends on the browser you use.

Another feature you may find useful is opening tabs in another window. A lot of your reading assignments may be links to other websites. I find it useful to open these links in another window, or tab of my web browser, so I do not lose my place in the course. To open a link in another tab or window, right click on the link and choose the appropriate option.

I also like the "Add to Reading List" list in the Safari web browser. Adding a website to a reading list is another way to bookmark the page so you can access it later to read.

EMAIL

Email is the primary way your enrollment counselor, student advisor, and instructors will communicate with you. Like using the Internet, I am assuming you know the basics of using email. We will discuss more about communicating through email in Chapter 6. For now, though, the most important thing to have is an email account and a way to check your email.

Most schools will set you up with a free student email account that you can use for all your school communication. If you already have a personal email account that you regularly check, you can set up your school account to forward to your personal account. That way, you don't have to check two different accounts.

If you do not have a personal account and want to set one up, there are several free options available, including the Google email service, Gmail. If you are a Mac user, check out iCloud email. Do a search online, and you will find many other options.

Once you have an email account, become familiar with how to write, send, and receive your email messages.

MICROSOFT OFFICE

You will need to be familiar with the apps in Microsoft Office or Office 365, as these are the foundation of productivity for nearly every aspect of academic and professional life. Most schools require you to submit assignments using Word, Excel, or PowerPoint, as appropriate. Before you invest in expensive add-on applications, check out the functionality and tools already built into these programs and save yourself money, as well as hours of time and frustration, in the process. The reference feature in Microsoft Word is a good example. Students often pay for add-ons to Word to help with formatting their papers, not knowing that Word already has this feature.

If you are unfamiliar with these programs, <u>GCFLearnFree. org</u> has tutorials on how to use the Internet, email, and many of the Microsoft Office programs. And they are free! If you invest the time to learn these skills now, you will have a much easier time getting started.

TEXTBOOKS

One of the biggest reasons I see students fail is because they do not get the course textbooks before class begins, if at all. In many cases, students are waiting for student loan money to be dispersed so they can purchase their textbooks. The problem with waiting for student loans is it may be several weeks into the class before they receive their funds. It is difficult to keep up with a course without the textbooks, and waiting until the third week of an accelerated, five-week class to purchase them is unreasonable and extremely unwise!

In some cases, students spend their student loan money on other things, such as food, gas, or medicine. I get that. Just before my wife, Beth, stopped out (she refuses to say, "dropped out") of college the first time, for a month, she lived on potatoes and the cheapest hot dogs she could find, trying to make ends meet. She did what she had to do to purchase her textbooks and other school materials.

Books can get expensive, and if you cannot afford them, you may have to wait to begin your classes. About three years into my time in the Army, I wanted to take college courses. And while the Army paid the tuition for my classes, I had to purchase the textbooks. Unfortunately, I did not have the money for them, so I held off registering for classes. I remember my mother asking me why I had not signed up for college classes. When I told her that I could not afford the books, she offered to pay for them. That was all I needed! I immediately signed up for classes.

Plan ahead by setting up a book fund for upcoming classes. Once your financial aid is disbursed, consider setting aside money for the next class. Each semester, add to your book fund to help offset the costs. This will help you to be ready when classes begin.

DO YOU NEED TEXTBOOKS?

In today's Internet information age, it may feel like spending big bucks on textbooks is a waste of money. I'm right there with you. When I tell my wife, Beth, that I need to purchase a book, she wants to know if I can find it at the library. I tease her that she is stingy, but the truth is, she is very wise when it comes to spending money. Our son-in-law doesn't help matters. He is more than happy to point out all the books his professors made him buy, only to be assigned a few pages out of them. Historically, that is all too often true in traditional campus-based classes. However, this is less likely to be true for online classes, which are created by a team of instructional designers, as opposed to a single professor.

Instructional designers are more conscious of the burden of purchasing textbooks. Because of this, they only require books that are actually used in the course. This makes it all the more important to study the assigned reading from the textbooks, as well as supplemental materials included in the course.

Many courses have a list of required books and suggested books for additional reading. To find out which books are required and which books are suggested, check your course syllabus. Many students ignore the list of suggested books for additional reading, but you should at least consider purchasing them, if you can. The suggested books can be very helpful in providing background information about the topic, or other tools, such as writing style guides. If you are unfamiliar with the writing expectations in college, a writer's guide may be very helpful to you. The bottom line is to have the required textbooks in hand before the first day of class. Do not expect any special considerations if you do not have them.

PAPER OR ELECTRONIC?

Many students ask me my opinion about electronic books or print versions. It is really a personal preference, but here are a few things to consider.

Some people are more comfortable using the old-fashioned print version of books. Not only do they get to hold it in their hands, but they also can mark them up with pens and highlighters and bookmark pages. They also look nice on a bookshelf. If you have seen any of my videos, you know I have several bookshelves full of books.

But electronic books have many advantages, too. Like a print book, you can highlight passages and bookmark pages. You may not get the feel of holding a book, but reading an eBook on a tablet has a very familiar look and feel. One of the biggest advantages of eBooks over print versions is you can search for words in the text. Can't remember where you read the passage on kinesthetic learning? Just search for the word *kinesthetic*, and you will find it very quickly.

Another advantage is eBooks are usually cheaper than the print version. I say *usually* because there are exceptions, but for the most part, they are less expensive.

If you ever find yourself in the position of needing to get a copy of your textbook quickly, save the cost of overnight shipping and purchase an electronic version of the book if it is available. When you buy an eBook at Amazon.com, you have immediate access to it on your Kindle, mobile device, and computer. You do not have to have a Kindle device, either; you can download the Kindle app for free on any computer or mobile device.

So, which do I prefer? Depends on what I need the book for. When I was in graduate school, I purchased the books I could in electronic form to take advantage of the search feature. If I am purchasing a book just to read for enjoyment and enlightenment, I typically get the print version.

There is no correct answer to the question. It is all about your personal preference. The choice might be made for you. Maybe you are fortunate enough to be at a school that uses open source materials that are free and available online. We are also seeing more schools providing the textbooks as part of the cost of tuition.

WHERE AND WHEN DO I PURCHASE THEM?

Many students automatically order them from the campus bookstore. If you have ample time and they have ample stock, then that's fine. More likely these days, the university bookstore can't keep up with the demand for traditional in-seat classes, let alone online courses. So, what do you do if they do not have your textbooks in stock?

When Beth was in graduate school, she was fortunate to find many of her required textbooks at a local university library (hence, the reason she always asks me if the library has a copy before purchasing a book). As a resident of the city, she could get a library card for the university and borrow all the books she needed. Some of the books were an edition older than what the syllabus called for, but she made it work. When this happened, she searched online to check what was new in the updated edition to ensure she wasn't missing anything vital. That is harder to do now because new editions address technology issues that weren't all that important before. You also have to be careful because your university may have updated the assignments to reflect changes in the book. If that is the case, you must get the latest edition or your grades might suffer as a consequence.

Another option is to order books and supplies from an online bookstore. Some offer student discounts. Not only can you shop for the best price, but you will also have the option of purchasing new or used books. In some cases, you can get electronic books (eBooks), which gives you immediate access to the book on your computer. Sometimes you can rent your textbooks. Another option is to find a digital version of the book you need that you can sample as a preview, which normally gives you access to the first chapter. This can be a good option while you wait for your print copy to arrive. While we cannot officially endorse all of these, here are a few places to get you started on your search for great deals.

- Amazon.com: Buy or rent print or Kindle eBook versions

- BookRenter.com

- CampusBookRentals.com

- Chegg.com

- eCampus.com

- Knetbooks.com

- Textbooks.com

Don't be afraid of doing your own search to see if your required book is available somewhere for free. Get reacquainted with your local library. Most have great websites making virtual visits possible. Many use www.OverDrive.com to check out eBooks and subscribe to several subscription-based databases with thousands of items accessible in digitized formats. You might be pleasantly surprised at what else you can find. Again, there are no guarantees. Here are a few places you may start your search with.

- Bartleby Library–Searchable collection of classic works (most published in the 20th century).

- Bookshare.org–free for qualified US students and schools, funded by the Office of Special Ed. Programs, US Department of Education.

- eServer.org–a growing online community where hundreds of writers, artists, editors, and scholars publish works as open archives, available free of charge to readers.

- Google Book Search–page images of millions of fully read-able public domain books, plus excerpts of many more. For better results, use the advanced search tool found at https://books.google.com/advanced_book_search.

- Hathi Trust Digital Library–a partnership of academic and research institutions, offering a collection of millions of titles digitized from libraries world-wide.

- <u>Internet Archive Lending Library</u>–a non-profit library of millions of free books, movies, software, music, websites, and more.

- <u>Playster.com</u>–an online subscription-based lending library that offers a one-month free trial.

- <u>Project Gutenberg</u>–electronic text of classic titles.

However you decide to acquire your textbooks, they are like any tool you need to succeed. Make it a priority to get them before your class begins.

The book you don't read won't help. ~ Jim Rohn

AVOID GETTING LOST IN [VIRTUAL] SPACE

In a traditional on-campus college setting, a formal orientation day is typically scheduled to introduce new students to the school and all the resources available to them. For the non-traditional student, that is not always the case, so you need to conduct your own orientation. If you skip out on this step, you risk missing vital resources that could help you succeed academically. Consider the online campus your new home and check it out.

Some prefer to jump in and learn as they go. But think about the last time you started a new job. Most likely, one of the first things to happen was you were given a tour of the place to become familiar with your surroundings and introduced to some of the key people you needed to know. You should begin your online education in the same way. Explore your virtual classroom and campus to become familiar with your surroundings and get to know who to contact for what and how to contact them.

Your academic advisor can help, but ultimately, it is your responsibility to log in to your school's LMS and get familiar with everything.

YOUR VIRTUAL CAMPUS

From the main dashboard of your LMS, nearly every school has a link to a student resources section. Start there. Check out the video tutorials, which can help you become an expert in navigating your way around the LMS. There may also be tutorials on writing and other study strategies.

Other things you will find include the Student Handbook, which will have all the policies and procedures you are expected to know. For example, get familiar with the policy for submitting late assignments. Is there a grace period to submit late assignments? If so, what is the penalty for submitting assignments late? You will also find information about extensions, plagiarism, and other academic policies.

Take a tour of the online library. There you will find tutorials on how to use the different databases for your research, how to request books, and other resources that will help you with your school work.

Make a note of other resources available to you such as technical support, tutoring, etc.

YOUR VIRTUAL CLASSROOM

Next, log in to your class and begin exploring what is available and where to find information. One of the first things you should do is look for the course syllabus. I suggest you download a copy or bookmark it so you can reference it quickly if you have any questions. The syllabus will give you a good idea of what to expect in the class, a list of the assignments, when they are due, and how many points they are worth. This information will help you in planning your schedule.

Check out everything on the course home page. Most courses are set up with designated divisions for modules, sessions, or weeks. Click through them and explore what is in store for you. Look at the list of the required reading and assignments due in the first week.

Also look at the grade book. Depending on the LMS, it may be called "Your Grades" or something similar. You should see a list of all the assignments and due dates. If you click on an assignment, you should see the grading expectations or rubric used to evaluate your assignments.

Other things you will find in your virtual classroom include the contact information for your instructor. Most of your communication will be done by email, but your instructor will normally include a phone number and office hours when you can reach him or her.

One of the most important things you will see in your virtual classroom is the Student Lounge or Cyber Café, Virtual Office, or something similar. This is a discussion forum where you can post questions about assignments and share information with your classmates. Your instructor may also post things to help you. I post my expectations for online discussions and other things to clarify what I require from assignments. One thing to keep in mind is the Student Lounge is not the place to ask about grades or other personal information. We will discuss more about this in another chapter.

Read all announcements your instructor posts. Many instructors will post an overview each week describing the assignments and information on how to best complete them. In addition, more and more instructors are posting video announcements. Take the time to view these, as they may include more information than what is provided in the written instructions. Watching a video from your instructor is also a good way to get to know them more than you would from a written announcement.

Conducting your own orientation will help you feel more comfortable in the online learning environment, and you will be more confident when it is time to begin.

MANAGE FOR SUCCESS

Managing our success is something we can all learn to do. In this section, we will discuss ways to manage your communication, time, and, most importantly, yourself.

The challenge is not to manage time,
but to manage ourselves.
~ Stephen Covey ~

COMMUNICATION CHANNELS

Effective communication is a multi-level, two-way street and your lifeline to academic success. As a student, you will communicate with your instructor, classmates, and other people such as your advisor and technical support.

On a broad level, the content in the course shell communicates all the basic information such as required course materials to read or view, assignment instructions, discussion forums, etc. However, you may receive other helpful information through announcements, posts to a discussion forum, and your school email account.

It is your responsibility to keep up with this information. With that in mind, a good rule of thumb is to check your email every day and log in to your course two to three days a week to make sure you don't miss anything new that is posted.

COMMUNICATION FROM YOUR INSTRUCTOR

Instructors generally communicate with their students in two ways. They post announcements with general information for the entire class and send email messages to individual students with specific information or feedback.

Announcements are used for several things. For instance, at the beginning of each week, many instructors post an announcement with an overview of activities and assignments for the week. Using short videos is becoming more common for this. Instructors may also post an announcement with general feedback and observations from the assignments he or she graded. Announcements are also used to alert students of changes, as well as to clarify expectations and assignment instructions. These are very important and ignoring them may affect your grade.

Unfortunately, this happens all too often. I have taught many of the courses I teach multiple times, and each time I do, I realize where some students will get stuck. To help avoid these sticky situations, I often post an announcement to the course home page or in the Student Lounge (a discussion area in the course to share information) with clarifications and suggestions for how to approach a particular assignment. Unfortunately, not every student reads these announcements, and in some cases, they miss a vital part of the assignment, which costs them points. It is up to you to check for updates and stay informed. Some LMSs will allow you to subscribe to the discussion forum, and when you do, you will be sent an alert when new items are posted. If you do not have this option, plan to check for new posts at least two or three times throughout the week.

Outside of the course shell, most of the communication between you and your instructor is done through email. You will be assigned a school email address, and this is where all your school-related communication will be sent. You may also have the option to forward your school email to your personal email. However you choose to set it up, it is your responsibility to check your email on a regular basis. I suggest you check it at least once a day. Read or not, you will be held accountable for any questions or deadlines contained in the messages.

COMMUNICATION TO YOUR INSTRUCTOR

As a non-traditional student, things come up that will throw off your schedule. You need to expect the unexpected and be prepared to communicate with your instructor when it happens.

For instance, if you know you are going to be late submitting an assignment, send an email to your instructor and let them know. You do not need to go into a lot of personal detail; just briefly tell them what happened and that you are going to be late with your assignment. Depending on your school's policy, you might avoid late penalties by arranging with your instructor to submit your assignment late. At the very least, it is a professional courtesy.

Many students use text messaging to communicate with friends and family, but unless your instructor specifically mentions that you can send them text messages, do not assume your instructor can receive them. I had a student who sent me multiple text messages over the course of two weeks, not realizing that the phone number she was sending them to was not a cell phone and, therefore, unable accept text messages. It was only after she sent me an email that we finally connected.

You may also find an application within the LMS that allows you to send messages. Before you depend on this application to communicate with your instructor, check with them to see if they use it. I have had students post a message to me, and I did not see it for several days.

Somewhere in your virtual classroom, your instructor posts his or her contact information. They may also tell you how they prefer you contact them and the best time to reach them. If they do not, send them an email and ask if they prefer email, messaging, or phone calls. Every instructor is different, so never make assumptions.

An important thing to keep in mind is your privacy. When you have questions about the feedback your instructor provides to you, it is important to keep this type of conversation private, in keeping within the guidelines of the <u>Family Educational Rights and Privacy Act (FERPA)</u>. Questions about your feedback or grades should never be posted in an open discussion, such as the Student Lounge, where your classmates can read it. When a student posts something like this to an open forum, I delete the post and send them a message reminding them of the need to keep this private and send them a response to their email address.

COMMUNICATION WITH YOUR CLASSMATES

Discussions are often asynchronous, which means there is no set time to meet or take part in the discussion; they are open for viewing and posting 24/7 during a set period of time, which is typically a week. Think of them like a closed social media group where your classmates can carry on collaborative online conversations. In a discussion, you will most likely be required to "create a thread" or post a response to the discussion prompt, and then your classmates can read and respond to you. These individual "conversations" are what make up the online class discussion. They can quickly become valuable study groups, and it pays to eavesdrop on every conversation in the discussion, not just those in your own thread. You never know when a comment made to a classmate's post will help you with your assignment.

TECHNICAL SUPPORT

I often receive email and phone calls from students telling me that they are having a technical problem and need help. Unfortunately, I cannot help a student who cannot connect to the Internet, or log in to the LMS, or a host of other technical difficulties. That is what technical support is for. They are trained to help you with these types of issues. When you have a technical problem, save yourself some time and frustration and call the Help Desk. They will get you up and running again.

If the issue is complicated and will take time to fix, by all means, contact your instructor and make them aware of your situation. They may not be able to fix the problem, but they should know if you are going to be late with an assignment.

I suggest having offline access to phone numbers and emails for at least the following three contacts: your academic advisor, your instructor, and the IT Help desk. Add them to your contacts on your smartphone. Having a print copy is ideal in case a storm disables your Internet connection or your computer crashes. You may need to give the information to someone to contact them for you if you have an accident or emergency health issue. Whatever the case may be, always have access to your instructor's email address and phone number. You never know when you may need it.

COMMUNICATION
COMPETENCE

This section is not just about following the rules for proper mechanics (spelling, punctuation, or grammar), although that does play a part. This section, rather, is about enhancing your reputation and being clearly understood by the person with whom you are trying to communicate. Good communication is one of the most important parts of being a successful online student, but one that is often ignored.

The essentials of academic communication mirror the essentials of business communication. What helps you get ahead in college is good practice for thriving in your future career. Some habits need to be ditched quickly because they scream *amateur!* With that said, here are some tips to help you be an effective communicator.

ALWAYS IDENTIFY YOURSELF

When you communicate with your instructor, use the same name you used when you registered for the class. If you go by another name such as a nickname, your instructor may not be able to identify you, and that may hold up the process of answering your email. Adding the course and section number is extremely helpful for instructors who teach multiple classes or at multiple schools.

Consider setting up a signature block to be automatically entered into email messages you send out, even if your name is part of your email address. That way, you never forget to include this act of common courtesy of clearly and completely identifying yourself. If friends think it's odd, they'll get over it. You're preparing to impact the world, and you need to look and act the part.

For instructors, student identification touches on privacy protection and potential legal issues related to that. This is federally regulated by the <u>FERPA</u>. Instructors can only discuss details about a student's work with the student enrolled in the course. If an instructor is unsure of who the email is from, they may not be able to provide you with the information you are seeking until they verify your identity. In addition to using the name that is on your instructor's student roster, some instructors may want you to provide your student identification number. Ask if you are not sure and follow their guidelines.

Failure to properly identify yourself can cost time and create a mountain of frustration for both student and instructor. Here is an example that occurred in one of my classes this past year.

One day, I received an email from a student asking a question about the grade she received on an assignment. The student did not identify herself or what class she was taking. There was a name listed in the email address, but the name did not appear on any of the rosters of my current courses. I sent her a reply asking her to please iden-tify herself.

On day two, an email arrived stating that her name was Jessica. There were two students by the name Jessica in two different classes. I sent a second reply asking Jessica to please provide her last name and what class she was in.

On day three, she sent a reply stating that she was in the history class and provided her last name. For the sake of this story, let's say it was Jones. None of the class rosters listed a Jessica Jones. I sent a third reply asking Jessica if she was sure she was in my class. Students do occasionally email the wrong instructor.

On day four of this exchange, her reply came with the added note that Jones was her married name. She was officially registered in the class under her maiden name, Jessica Smith. With that information, I could finally, verify who she was and answer her question.

If she had properly identified herself in her first email message, it would not have taken four days to answer her question. When a typical session is only seven days long, four days may be too late to put the answer into action.

TIMING IS IMPORTANT

Do not wait until the last minute to send your instructor an email with a question. And, please do not get impatient waiting for a response. Instructors are real people, not a robotic head living online 24/7. Most schools expect instructors to respond to email messages within 24 hours, and on weekends, they are allowed 48 hours.

With that in mind, give your instructor the time to respond to you before you send another email with the same question. I know you may think it is urgent and you are waiting for an answer, but three messages all in one day with the same question sends the wrong message.

If your situation is truly an emergency, pick up the phone and call your instructor. If you get their voicemail, leave a detailed message. At a minimum, identify yourself, provide good contact information, and summarize your question or message. Make sure you are loud enough to be heard and speak clearly. Don't rush. You might be surprised at how many messages I receive that I cannot hear or understand. If the voicemail cuts you off, you can always call back and finish up in a second message.

Factor in giving the instructor time to respond, and keep the instructor's office hours in mind. Typically, instructors will respond to you in 24 hours or less, but if you send a message on the weekend, it may be up to 48 hours before you hear back from them.

As the old saying goes, lack of prior planning on your part does not constitute an emergency on my part. Avoid last-minute panic messages by previewing your assignments early in the week. That way, if you have any questions, you have plenty of time to send an email to your instructor and get a response before you begin writing your assignment.

TIPS FOR WRITING A GOOD EMAIL

Savvy students use the subject line like a media headline—a flag waving for attention. Instructors are like people everywhere and tend to respond quicker and better when they see a subject line that is specific and concrete. Avoid vague outbursts of frustration, like "Help!" or "hey." It may feel satisfying to say, but it might not get you very far. Everyone says that and now your plain flag is just like all the others, and your email is buried in a list of hundreds of shouts for "help." Blank subject lines can get overlooked, too. There is no flag waving at all. Also, consider including the name of the assignment you have a question about, especially if that helps indicate that your request for information is particularly time sensitive.

Use a semi-formal to formal tone. Not only does it better represent your relationship with the recipient, but it also conveys respect. Save informalities for close friends and relatives. There are many ways to sound pleasant and professional, and now is as good a time as any to practice that skill.

Many times, you might be feeling very frustrated, which is why you are writing. Take a deep breath and read through your message before sending it. If you have time, set it aside and revise it with a fresher attitude. Delete any snippy, snarky, or passive-aggressive phrases that can easily creep in when you are frustrated or upset. I have received these types of messages, and I often want to ask my student if they realize I am the one grading their assignment. If it isn't how you would speak to your boss, who pays your salary, don't say it that way to your instructor, who grades your assignments.

Clear and concise is nice. Long-winded wordiness is likely to get skimmed over. Always lead with your need. This is a good habit, whether you are communicating in a discussion forum, email, or otherwise. Avoid including cutesy quotes or rambling into a soliloquy of some kind, as they can interfere with the meaning of your message.

I remember one student who sent me an email every week with questions about the assignment due that week (which was good!), but they were very long and detailed. He would tell me way more than I needed to know, and the question he wanted answered was buried in the fourth or fifth paragraph. In some cases, I could not figure out what he was asking because the message was so long that it covered several topics. I asked him to be more concise, but I guess he liked to write because his messages did not change. In the working world, his messages would probably be ignored.

Avoid YELLING, which is typing in all capital letters, or excessive use of punctuation. It doesn't matter if your intentions were simply to show enthusiasm. In professional circles, using ALL CAPS is often viewed as being overly emotional and may earn you the label of a drama king or queen.

Other graphical devices that are seen as unprofessional include texting shorthand (or text-ese, as I like to call it), excessive exclamations, italics, etc. Use complete words and sentences, it will help in conveying your message without any confusion.

Emails should be easy to read. Avoid unprofessional fonts and favor the boring (but highly readable) ones, instead. These include Arial, Calibri, or Times New Roman in 10- to 12-point type. As for the color of the font, black is best. Colorful backgrounds can delay downloading, depending on the recipient's connection speed, so it is best to avoid these, as well.

Presentation sets a tone and sloppy mechanics often detract from the meaning. Use spelling and grammar check tools. They are often built right in with the email software you are using. Never be in such a hurry (or unmotivated) to ignore this step. I have received messages that were so poorly written that I could not understand the message or the question asked. When I receive a message like that, I have to send a reply asking them to restate their question, which only delays the student getting an answer. Using proper grammar and spelling not only helps you look professional, but it also often helps catch mistakes that can change the meaning of the message.

Mastering the art of good communication etiquette doesn't require crafting a masterpiece each time. That could take forever. If you follow these tips, you'll be off to a great start.

DEVELOPING A DIGITAL PRESENCE

Related to communication in an online class is your digital presence. Your digital presence tells a lot about you and often creates an impression about who you are as a person. It can also establish a trust factor. As a student, your digital presence is formed from how people see you online; namely, your email address and avatar. A professional email address and good avatar can help your instructor and classmates get a glimpse of you and establish a sense of familiarity and trust.

WHAT DOES YOUR DIGITAL ADDRESS SAY ABOUT YOU?

Let's start with your email address. As a student, you will have one assigned to you, typically based on your name. Perhaps you have everything forwarded to your personal email, and that is what you use to communicate with others. As we discussed in a previous chapter, that is perfectly okay, if that works best for you.

Just remember that your email address is the first thing your instructor sees from you. In many cases, it is the first impression they will have about you. With that in mind, think about what your email address says about you. Is it a professional-looking email address, such as john.smith@anyemail.com? Or is it one made of cutesy, sexy, vulgar, or nonsensical words, such as hotmama@anyemail.com? Email addresses like this can be confusing, at best, and offensive, at worst. If you choose to use your personal email to communicate with your instructor, consider creating a new email account that makes a good first impression.

WHAT DOES YOUR AVATAR SAY ABOUT YOU?

You may also have the option of uploading a picture of yourself in your school profile. This is called an avatar, which is an icon or figure representing a particular person in computer games, Internet forums, etc. In the case of an online class, it should be a picture of you. Each time you post a response to a discussion, your avatar will appear, which is a great way for your instructor and classmates to get to know a bit about you.

Here are a couple of suggestions to keep in mind if you choose to create a school avatar. First, keep in mind the size of the picture. In the course, your picture will appear as a small square of about a half inch or so. Keep that in mind when choosing a picture. Use a close-up short or crop the photo, so everyone can see what it is. Second, choose a picture that makes it easy to identify you—choose a picture of you! Many students will post a picture of their baby or their puppy. While this is very cute, it is not you. Many students like to use a family picture or a something with several people in it, and it is not always easy to figure out who in the picture is the student. Plus, that tiny size means none of the people in the picture are really viewable anyway (see first tip).

Whatever you choose to use for an email address and avatar, keep it professional. Remember, in an online course, this is how people will see you.

COUNT THE COST:
TIME MANAGEMENT

Pursuing a college degree is a major commitment, and taking classes online is no different than taking them in-seat. It just makes exactly where and when more flexible.

Time is a coin with two sides: quality and quantity, and it takes both to be a successful student. The challenge for many students is they do not have an abundance of time, so it is all the more important to manage time so that it is quality time.

Many students taking online courses are non-traditional students, and they have many priorities in their life, such as family, work, and church, to name a few. Going back to school is one more thing to add to the list, which is why it is important to give your school work due consideration when scheduling your time.

HOW MUCH TIME IS NEEDED?

Many online courses are five to eight weeks long. This is referred to as an accelerated format. A good rule of thumb is to schedule 8-12 hours each week for your academic tasks. You may need to add more time if you find the subject matter is more challenging. You will have course materials to read and review, discussions to participate in, papers to write, and, perhaps, quizzes to take. All of this takes time, and you need to plan for it. Start as early in the week as you can to allow breathing space because life happens and issues almost never come at a convenient time.

One thing some students neglect to do is carve out the extra time needed to complete their school work. They assume they can squeeze it in with all the other activities and responsibilities they have. This is a big mistake and often ends up with the student falling behind, and in some cases, failing a course. When considering all the expense and effort involved with going to college, it needs to be a priority.

One way to carve out the time needed for school work is to take a break from extra-curricular activities. Take a season or two off from the softball team, take a break from the church choir. This allows you to dedicate your best efforts to this important academic season of your life.

Another thing you can do is recruit supportive friends and family to help where they can so you can devote the time needed for your studies. Perhaps you can arrange for someone to pick the kids up from school or take them to the park. Things like this will create some of the time you need.

Remember, this is a relatively short-term season, not a lifetime commitment. You will be able to pick those activities back up before you know it.

SET YOUR PRIORITIES

Be proactive in your time management. Schedule your academic work time as a high-priority commitment on your calendar. Most of us have seen the jar-of-life illustration, where big rocks, little rocks, and sand represent the many things that take up our time. To fit everything in the jar, you have to first put in the big rocks, which represent the important commitments in your life. Things like time with your family and your job are big rocks. Then, you can add the little rocks, which represent the less-important commitments. These might include recreational activities. Once you have the big and small rocks in the jar, you can add in the sand to fill the jar. The sand represents things that take time, but are not all that important. Your schoolwork needs to be one of the big rocks that must be put in the jar before you add little rocks or sand. If you try to put it in later, you may find that it does not fit.

In one of my online discussions I have with my students, I ask them a question about when they do their homework. Do they schedule their study time in the morning, afternoon, evening, or whenever they have time? There is no correct answer to this question, but there is definitely one incorrect answer; and that is whenever they have time.

The point of my discussion is to encourage everyone to schedule their study time at a regular time that works for them. When they do, it becomes a habit. Those who do not schedule a regular time, but choose to do their homework whenever they have time, are setting themselves up to fail. Failing to make school work a priority means other things will always come up that have a higher priority (like the sand that fills up the jar).

SET UP YOUR SCHEDULE

When planning your schedule, plan to meet three main course-based commitments each week: 1) reading and reviewing of course materials, 2) regular engagement with instructor and classmates, and 3) working on assignments.

Commit to logging into your course daily, or at least three times a week to check for new announcements and discussion posts and engaging with your academic peers in the discussion forums.

When you begin a course, write the due dates for all your assignments on your calendar, including when your initial response to a discussion is due, which is normally in the middle of the week. At many schools, courses open online a few days or even a week prior to the official start date, so you have plenty of time to set up your schedule.

Consider using an app on your smartphone to help manage and keep track of your schedule. One option I highly recommend is the istudiez app. This app works on both iOS and Windows, PCs, and Macs. It also integrates with your calendar on your computer and other devices. In istudiez, you enter all your assignments, the due dates, the points each one is worth, and other information to help you stay on top of things. With all that information, it keeps you up to date with your grade average and schedule of classes. I used this app in my last few years of school, and it was a great tool. For more information, go to istudentpro.com or look it up in your app store.

Once you have added all the due dates for your assignments on your calendar, back-date time needed to review course materials and work on those assignments. How much time is needed depends on the course materials required and the length and scope of assignments. Whether the course follows a traditional 15-week schedule or is accelerated into five, six, eight, or ten weeks should also be considered. Be realistic when factoring in your familiarity with the topics as well as your abilities and skills for learning.

SUGGESTED SCHEDULE

Assuming your academic week begins on a Monday, here is an overview of a suggested schedule.

When the Course Opens:

- Read the Overview and Syllabus.

- Read any welcome announcements posted by the instructor.

- Set up your calendar with alerts for assignment due dates.

- Scan each week's overview and assignment instructions to become familiar with what is expected of you in the course.

- If you have questions, post them in the designated discussion forum, which may be called Virtual Office or Student Lounge.

- Get a head start reading and reviewing course materials.

During the Week:

Monday

- Check for announcements and instructional updates.

- Review the assignments due this week, so you know what is expected when you read your course reading assignments.

- Begin reading all the reading assignments for the week.

Tuesday

- Complete the reading assignments.

Wednesday

- Write and post your response to the discussion forum assignment.

Thursday

- Read your classmates' posts in the discussion forum and post a reply to at least one.

- If you have not already done so, begin working on the other assignments due this week.

Friday

- Submit your assignments.

- Read and respond to at least one other of your classmates' posts in the discussion.

- Review instructions for the next week's assignments (Discussions and Dropbox).

- Read/view course materials for next week.

If you can keep up with a schedule like this, you will have the weekends for other activities, or to catch up with your assignments, if needed.

WORK SMARTER

How do successful students complete their work twice as fast with half the effort? They follow most, if not all, of these easy steps. First, as I mentioned above, look at your study time as one of the large rocks in a jar. Successful students keep their academic tasks as a priority. Second, find a place to study which provides solitude in a distraction-free environment equipped with the proper tools and tailored for your personality. Remember to shut off your phone or at least mute it, so you are not interrupted each time someone posts something new to Facebook. If listening to music helps, create a study playlist through your favorite music app. For best results, choose music that is lyrics-free or sung in a foreign language you do not understand. Third, take care of yourself. If your study time is more than an hour or so, schedule regular breaks. Also, remember to take care of yourself, eating right and getting plenty of exercise. Finally, build momentum. Do the easy tasks first and divide difficult projects into easier chunks of time. Following these guidelines will put you in control of your time and keep you on top of your school commitments.

TAKE RESPONSIBILITY

As a student in a traditional educational setting, if you need help, you have the instructor, teaching assistant, classmates, and other resources readily available. In a non-traditional format, you have the same resources available to you, but you must be more pro-active to get the help you need. This distinction often throws students off track, so let's look at what it means to "Take Responsibility."

FILL THE GAP

There are two types of enrollments in education. In traditional education, you fill out an application, and your admission is determined based on your grades from previous college work or high school and your college entrance exams, such as the ACT or SAT exams. The school admissions officials look at these to determine if you are qualified and ready for the rigors of study.

Open enrollment, on the other hand, does not consider these things. You fill out an application, show that you have a high school diploma or GED, and you are accepted into the program of study. There is no consideration given to previous college work, high school grade point average, or college entrance exams. It is assumed that you are ready and able to begin class.

With that in mind, the first thing you are responsible for is to fill in any gaps you may have in your education. These gaps may be a lot of different things, but the two I see most often are gaps in writing skills and study skills. Many non-traditional schools provide resources to help you fill in these gaps, but it is up to you to determine what help you may need and to seek it out. Let's look at a couple of examples.

If you have been out of school a long time, you may need a crash course in study skills, such as understanding the best approach to reading a textbook. Do you just turn to page one and start reading? No. There is more to it than that. We will cover reading in Chapter 9.

Have you thought about where and when you are going to study? Choosing a place with as few distractions as possible is best. Everyone has their own preferences as to what works best for them. Here are a few things to consider.

Have a desk or table to spread out your books, notes, and laptop or PC. Lighting is also important. Some students like to work in a dark room with a lamp. That way, they only focus on what is lit and ignore other distractions hidden in the dark.

If it is possible, I suggest you work in a room where no one will bother you. Set up a small desk or table in a room where you can close the door. If you have a large family and must work in a room shared with others, let everyone know that you are studying and how much you appreciate them keeping it down.

Students have told me that they try to study in the same room where their kids or spouse watches television. I don't know about you, but I would end up watching whatever is on the TV instead of doing my homework; even if it is not a show I like! The sound coming from the TV is very distracting, too. If you have to study in the same room where everyone watches TV, set up a quiet time for studying. During this time, everyone needs to agree to keep the TV off and keep other distractions to a minimum.

The bottom line is you need a quiet place to study where no one will bother you or distract you. This is one of the reasons why it is important that everyone in your household be on board with your going to college. Everyone must make sacrifices to some degree.

Another gap that is common is writing skills. Writing is one of the primary ways you will exhibit your knowledge and application of the subject of the course, and you need to have some basic writing skills. Those of you who did well in high school probably have these skills and may just need a refresher on the basics of academic writing. In Chapter 11, I discuss a few strategies in writing that you may find useful.

If you do not have a grasp on basic grammar and academic writing, you may need to invest time in acquiring some of these skills. Many non-traditional schools have online learning centers or student resources available to you. There you will find tutorials on basic writing and style. You may even find people in the lab to help you via online chats or phone calls.

Whatever the gap in your education may be, it is your responsibility to fill those gaps as best you can.

DO THE WORK

This may seem like an obvious statement, but it is worth mentioning. There is a common misconception that an online education does not require much effort. The thinking is a student should receive a good grade simply because they did the work. In other words, the grade is based on attempt. Unfortunately, that is not how it works. To earn a good grade, a student must meet certain standards and expectations.

Granted, in the past, there were educational institutions that were known as "diploma mills." If you paid the tuition, you would pass the course and eventually graduate. Things have changed. With the regional accrediting process, colleges and universities must meet certain standards and expectations, and pay to play is no longer acceptable.

What does this mean to you? You must do the work. Many of the online courses you will take are the same as a course you would take in a classroom on campus. You have the same reading assignments, same writing assignments, etc. You are essentially taking the same course as you would if you were attending the course on campus. That means you will have homework to complete, discussions to participate in, and papers to write and submit for a grade. If you do not do the work, you will fail the course, plain and simple.

Recently, I received an email from a student asking if he was going to pass the class. When I looked back at his grade book, I shook my head and thought to myself, "How does he expect to pass the course when he did not submit five assignments?" The hard thing for me was seeing that he did submit a couple of those assignments, but they were submitted after the grace period allowed by the late policy. I had no choice but to post a zero for the assignment, even though he completed and submitted it.

This brings to mind two things. First, you should not expect to pass a class if you do not submit the assignments. You can probably survive if you miss one or two, but if you are missing more than that, you may need to reconsider your priorities. Second, if you have to ask if you are going to pass the class, you are not paying enough attention to what is going on. Setting up your schedule and using apps like iStudiez will help you to manage yourself and your class.

TRACK YOUR PROGRESS

Something I was taught as a young noncommissioned officer in the United States Army was no one was more interested in my success than me. The point of this advice was that it was up to me to ensure my personnel records were up to date. This advice is applicable to students, too.

When it comes to your success as a student, no one is more interested than you. Your enrollment counselor will do all they can to ensure that you dot all the i's and cross all the t's of your application. Your student advisor will do all they can to ensure you take the courses you need to complete your degree, but they may have two hundred other students to care for, and there is only so much time in the day. Ultimately, it is up to you to ensure your enrollment counselor and student advisor have all the paperwork they need to keep your application and records up to date and complete. Your instructor is also interested in your completing their course successfully, but again, it is ultimately up to you.

As you have read in this book, there are many things that you have to keep up with as a student taking online courses. And it may seem a bit overwhelming. Even with all the support and help that is out there, you are ultimately responsible for ensuring you have all these tools.

DON'T GET BEHIND!

Every course I have taught has at least one required textbook, and there are reading assignments to complete each week. As we discussed in Chapter 3, purchasing your textbooks is something you need to be prepared to do. I can't tell you how many students have sent me an email in the middle of the first week telling me that they cannot afford to purchase their textbooks, and they want an extension to complete their first assignments until the next payday when they are able to purchase their books. You are responsible for acquiring your textbooks before class begins so that you can complete the reading assignments and be prepared for the assignments due the first week.

Another factor that must be considered is the length of the course. Most of the classes I teach are only five weeks long. When a student asks for an extension of the assignments due in the first week, they are essentially creating a four-week class. When a student asks for an extension, regardless of the reason, I always stress the importance that they catch up with their assignments as soon as possible and complete the assignments due the next week on time. It is very easy for a student to get behind in the first week, and then be behind in the following weeks. They put themselves in the position of always being late.

Speaking of late assignments, every school has a policy about accepting late assignments, and instructors are expected to adhere to the policy. Typically, you will have points deducted for each day your assignment is late. It could be as much as 10% per day. This happened to me once. I was three days late turning in a paper, and even though I earned an "A" for my work, I received a "C" for a grade because of the deduction of points. Ouch! That one late paper kept me from earning an "A" in the class.

Sometimes there is no getting around it. Things come up, such as being called out of town for work, or a sick child that needs extra loving and care. When it does, let your instructor know as soon as you can and ask them for an extension. Most instructors will do all they can to help you out.

Even if it is due to nothing more than poor time management, always let your instructor know you are going to be late. When you do, it shows initiative and personal responsibility. I know many instructors who will give a student a break on late penalties if they just contact them and are honest about their situation.

The bottom line is to only ask for the time you need. As I said above, it is easy to get behind, and then difficult to catch up. With that in mind, you do not want to ask for more time than you need.

Something else to consider when asking for extra time to submit an assignment is when you will receive your feedback. Like you, your instructors have busy lives. They have jobs, family responsibilities, and participate in extra-curricular activities. Most instructors are adjunct instructors, which means they probably have a full-time job in their career field and they teach part-time at colleges and universities. This means they have to schedule and plan their time, just like you do.

When it comes to grading, most instructors schedule the time to grade each of the assignments. They are required to have all assignments graded and returned to their students usually a couple of days before the next assignment is due. For instance, let's say a paper was due on Sunday evening for Unit 1, and the next paper is due next Sunday for Unit 2. The instructor should have the paper you submitted for Unit 1 graded and returned to you by Friday of Unit 2, so you have a couple of days to review and apply any corrections and suggestions to the next assignment due on Sunday.

When a student turns in a late assignment, the instructor may have already graded the assignments that were submitted on time. Remember the old adage, "An emergency on your part does not constitute an emergency on my part"? Well, that saying applies here, too. If you submit an assignment late, your instructor will do their absolute best to grade and return it to you as soon as they can. Just keep in mind that you may have missed the time he or she set aside for grading, and now they have to carve out additional time to grade your late assignment. It may be Saturday morning, which means you won't get it back 48 hours before the next assignment is due on Sunday.

ACHIEVE SUCCESS

I wish I could say grades don't matter, but they do. They contribute to your GPA, which is used for financial aid and admission to graduate school if you choose to go further with your education. There are a few jobs that still ask for your GPA during interviews, but in the larger scheme of things, few people care all that much. What employers really want to know is what you learned and can you keep improving. That's why successful students go for growth over grades. If you build on growth, the grades will come.

With that in mind, here are a few strategies to help you achieve success in your education.

Sometimes you win. Sometimes you learn.
~ John C. Maxwell ~

READING

In an online class, there is usually a list of reading assignments that need to be completed each week. It may be several chapters out of a textbook, along with other articles, websites, or posts. It is tempting to ignore the reading assignments and move on to the other assignments. Don't fall into that bad habit. Your assignments are based on the required reading, and your instructor will want to see evidence of your understanding and comprehension of the material.

If it has been some time since you have done any sort of academic reading, or perhaps you have never done this sort of reading, don't panic. It takes a bit of work, but with practice, it becomes easier. Trust me.

READING STRATEGIES

Here are some tips on reading for comprehension.

First, when you receive the book and open it up for the first time, look over the table of contents and read the introduction. This will help to understand the overall purpose and focus of the book.

Second, review the assignments due this week. Wait, I thought we were talking about reading the textbook? Stick with me; this is an important step. When you read through the assignments that are due, you will know what to look for in your assigned readings. If you read the textbook without knowing, you will end up reading it again when you sit down to write out your discussion posts or papers. Looking over the assignments first will save you time. As you read your textbook, you will recognize key points that you will want to reference in your assignments.

Next, when you begin your assigned reading, do the same as you did when you received your textbook, but on a smaller scale. Turn to the chapter you are going to read and look over the section headings, pictures, tables, and other such things. Look for key words and their definitions. These are often placed in the margins and easy to find.

Now that you are familiar with the overall content read the chapter. Highlight key concepts and ideas that are related to the assignments you will complete this week. Write down any questions you think of so you can refer back to them. When you have completed the reading, look over your questions and see if you can answer them. If not, send your instructor an email and ask him or her for clarification.

Another thing I highly recommend is to not leave your reading assignments until the same day you sit down to write your discussion posts and papers. Complete your reading early in the week, and then give it a day to percolate in your mind. I cannot tell you how many times I have read something, but did not fully under-stand it until the next day. I call it pondering. I complete the reading assignment and then ponder on it for a day or two as I consider how it applies to the other assignments. Then, when I sit down to write a paper, I have a better understanding of what I want to write.

OTHER THINGS TO CONSIDER

Some courses will ask you to take a self-graded quiz asking you to mark how much of the reading assignment you completed. Most stu-dents will answer this question honestly, so this adds incentive to complete all the required reading each week.

There are several reasons why you should always complete the required reading assignments. The first has to do with criti-cal thinking. Whether you are writing a paper or a response to an online discussion, you should always include references to academic sources to support your thoughts and ideas. For example, you may write a statement that says Abraham Lincoln is considered one of the greatest presidents in our history. You may think this to be a true statement, but by itself, it is just an opinion. When you add a refer-ence to something you have read as a way of supporting that state-ment, it is now a substantiated opinion. In other words, it is not just your opinion, but based on facts and observations you have made in your research.

Many students take shortcuts and do a search on the Internet for a reference to support their opinion. The sources they find online may be good, but they do not come from the textbook for the course. This can lead to writing a paper that is slightly off topic or written from a different perspective. I see this a lot. A student writes a good paper, but instead of relying on their textbook for their informa-tion, they take a shortcut and more times than not, miss the point of the assignment. It is for that reason that I recommend to students that they always begin with their textbook, and then if they want to include additional support or provide an alternative perspective from a good online source, go ahead. Just don't ignore your textbook for the sake of making it easy.

Another reason to complete all your reading assignments is a financial one. Most of you who are reading this book are investing a significant amount of money into your education, and you want to get the most value from it that you can. You might say you want to get the most bang for your buck. Part of the investment in your education is purchasing textbooks, and as many of you probably have come to realize, this can be an expensive investment. To get the most out of your investment, it makes sense to get the most you can from the textbooks that you paid good money for.

Another reason is to learn as much as you can from each of your classes. You may say that your reason for going to college is to get the credentials you need for that promotion you want or to be qualified to work in a specific career field, but there is more to it than that. When you have the credentials, that implies you also have the knowledge to back up those credentials. You may be qualified for your chosen field on paper, but do you also have the knowledge that is expected? Since you are investing in your education, it makes sense to get as much out of it as you can, and that includes reading all the required reading assignments; not just checking off another item on your to-do list each week, but to learn new information that you can apply to your assignments now, and your career later.

A QUICK STORY

To put this into perspective, let me share with you an email conversation I recently had with one of my students. This student was the first to post an initial response to an online discussion. While it was very well thought out, he did not include any reference to our reading assignments to support his thoughts. Since this was the first discussion in our class, I posted a reply asking him what he read in our assignments that supported his thoughts.

My student sent me an email apologizing for not including support and then explained that he had a good working knowledge of the topic and confessed that he did not do all the required reading that week before posting his response to the discussion.

In my response, I told him I appreciated his posting early in the week, but since he was the first, he inadvertently set the tone for the discussion. That is why I asked about what he read as a response to his post; I wanted everyone to see that this is an important part of a good academic discussion.

I then explained that in an academic setting, we must always give support to back up our thoughts and ideas and not depend upon our own understanding. It helps to ensure we are not reading too much into the subject of the assignment or taking it out of context.

I then concluded with one more thing to think about. We want to learn as much as we can about the subject matter of the course. Otherwise, why would we invest the money in an education? With that in mind, if we only depend on what we already know, we are robbing ourselves of the value of the class. Reading our required assignments teaches us new things and perhaps give us a different perspective that we may not have had prior to reading the assignment.

CONCLUSION

Referencing your course readings in your assignments is one way to get the most bang for your buck in your education. If you take shortcuts and only refer to things you already know or reference books you have already read, you are not cheating the system; you are cheating yourself!

Perhaps the biggest reason to include support from your textbook is it shows your instructor that you have read, understand, and can apply what you read to your assignments. As we discuss in another chapter, your writing is the primary way of determining your level of understanding the topic. If you do not complete the required reading each week and apply it to your assignments, it is difficult for your instructor to make that determination.

So, as you can see, it is important to read all the required reading assignments. It will make a difference in your learning experience.

ONLINE DISCUSSIONS

Online discussions, sometimes referred to as threaded discussions, are designed to supplement your learning through an interactive discussion with your instructor and classmates. If you have ever taken a course that met in a classroom, you may remember the discussions as one of the best opportunities for learning. Online discussions should be approached with the same attitude. Here are a few things to consider in making your online discussions a good experience and earn a good grade.

Grades for discussions typically focus on three areas: timing, interactivity with peers, and of course content. As I said, in many ways, they replicate the in-class discussions, but they take place over several days. It is easy to take the attitude of just completing another requirement, but when you do, you won't learn as much or earn as good a grade as you could. Approach your discussions as an opportunity to discuss the topic with your classmates.

Many find it helpful to subscribe to discussions, so they receive an alert when new posts are made. This may be forum-wide or individual threads, depending on how your school or the instructor has it set up. Definitely subscribe, if you can, to any forums where you and your classmates can post general course and assignment-specific questions. As I wrote in Chapter 5, it may make a difference in your grades!

TIMING AND PARTICIPATION

It is good practice to post early and post often. Posting early gives others more time to respond to you. It also allows the discussion to go deeper and gives you the opportunity to get to know each other better.

A good and profitable discussion includes three types of posts made throughout the week: an initial response, replies to your classmates, and replies back to your classmates' posts to you.

The initial response to a discussion should be your first post each week. Typically, you will have a due date to post your initial response. This can vary by school. In my experience, your initial response is due on Wednesday, Thursday, or Friday, leaving the rest of the week to read and reply to your classmates before the due date.

Once you have posted your initial response to the discussion, you should then read through your classmates' posts and choose one or two which you will respond to. In most schools, you will be required to respond to at least two of your classmates, but you are free to respond to as many as you like. Your responses must be posted by the second due date for the assignment, which is typically at the end of the week.

The third type of post is your reply back to the person who responded to your initial response. Many times, your classmates will ask you for clarification or ask a question, and they will appreciate and feel valued when you reply back to their response to your initial post. Part of your grade for participation may include whether you respond to these posts. I encourage my students to respond as a way of taking the discussion to the next level.

Related to the third type of post is replying to your instructor. He or she may ask you a question about your initial response or make a comment about something you wrote. It is good practice to always respond to your instructor.

As I said, the due date for your response to everyone is the end of the week. Asynchronous discussions allow flexibility for you to post when it is most convenient, but don't wait until late at night on the last day of the discussion to post a response to your classmates. When you do, it is like giving your response to an empty classroom because everyone else has already left the room. Where is the value in that? It is better to post your responses to your classmates a day or two before the discussion ends. That way there is time for them to read and respond back to you.

BEST PRACTICES TO FOLLOW:

1. Post your initial response by day 3 of the academic week. This gives you enough time to read through the reading assignments and ponder them for a day or so, as I described in Chapter 9.

2. Post your peer responses by day 5 of the academic week.

3. Post any replies back to peer responses by midnight on day 7 or the end of the academic week.

CONTENT DEVELOPMENT

Discussions are an opportunity to provide evidence that you have read, reflected on, and can apply the course materials as related to the learning objectives for the week. It is a chance to explore areas you may not quite understand and collaboratively learn them with your classmates. Posts should be constructive, coherent, and follow the standard conventions for college level writing, so others understand what you are saying. Remember that since your classmates cannot see you, as they would in a classroom, it is important to write out your posts in such a way that can be fully understood by others because there is no body language to help them interpret it.

BEST PRACTICES TO REMEMBER.

Correct (spelling, grammar, and formatting): Your discussion posts reflect your thoughts and ideas concerning the topic of the discussion prompt. Therefore, you should do your best to present your thoughts in the best way possible, which includes proper grammar and spelling. With that in mind, I suggest you write your thoughts in a Microsoft Word document so you can do a spelling and grammar check. These tools are more thorough than the spell check in any Internet browser.

Clear (language, style, and meaning): In the interest of clarity, a good habit is to restate the question as an opening statement–not to be confused with copying the question at the beginning of the initial post. When you restate the question into an opening statement, it helps to set the stage for your comments. It also helps to put your response in context. For example, say the question for the discussion is, "To what degree are you living out your vocation in life, and if you are not, what are the barriers that are preventing you from doing so?" You can rephrase this question into an opening statement like this, "As I reflect on Smith's views of vocation, I was reminded of…"

See the difference? Rather than listing the question and then the answer, it is much better to write out your response in this way. It is the beginning of a well-composed paragraph.

Complete (Referenced material): Include a reference to the reading assignments you have read for the week. Adding support from your textbook adds credibility to your thoughts and ideas, and it shows your instructor that you have read the material and can apply it to the assignment. This may or may not be applicable to all the discussions in your class

Constructive: Be on topic for the purpose of the discussion as it relates to the week's learning objectives. Evaluate and analyze course materials supported by insight, opinion, and additional information.

GRADING DISCUSSIONS

Here are some examples of how your post may be graded:

> **A-level work:** Deeply informed opinion–sound reasoning supported by deeper study/research of the topic (citing high-quality and credible sources);

> **B-level work:** Lightly-informed opinion–sound reasoning supported by personal experience or observation;

> **C-level work:** Opinion–personal preference or belief statement only;

> **D-level work:** Pointless remark–based on unsound reasoning (fallacy), or resorts to empty, abstract, or philosophically rhetorical questions that do not advance the topic-focused intent of the discussion.

OTHER TIPS

Write your post in Word, and it will save you time if you have to repost your response because of a technical glitch. Having to write a 300-word post that is well thought out and referenced is not easy. Save yourself some trouble and always save your discussion posts in a Word document, and then copy and paste each post into the comment box of the discussion.

When posting your initial response, be sure to click on the "Create Thread" link at the top of the discussion rather than responding to someone else's post. This makes it easier to follow your particular thread.

When posting, please be respectful of your fellow students' opinions and thoughts, and keep to the topic of discussion. It is very easy to go off on a tangent and get into a debate over politics and other such topics that are irrelevant to the discussion. If an instructor views a comment that is disrespectful or inflammatory, they may delete the thread from the discussion.

Review the Online Discussion Rubric to ensure you met all the requirements for the assignment.

ONE LAST THING

Occasionally, a student will send me an email asking why their classmates do not respond to their post. In my experience, there are three reasons why this happens. The first reason is poor writing skills or lack of clarity. The second is the post is too far off topic. The student wrote a good post, but it was not tied in with the context of the topic. And the third reason is the student wrote an excellent post and included good references to the reading, but it is too long and perhaps a bit complex. The instructor may appreciate the depth of the post, but it may go over the head of their classmates. This is not always a bad thing, but it can intimidate some students.

You will find online discussions to be one of the best things about online education. Rather than feeling like your instructor is putting you on the spot when he or she asks you a question in a class discussion, you have time to think about what you want to say and prepare a well thought out response.

11

WRITING STRATEGIES

Your writing is the primary way an instructor determines what you know and understand about a topic. Because of this, it is important that you put your best effort into your writing. Here are a few strategies to help you.

TAKE YOUR TIME!

The first thing you need to do is to take your time. Many students sit down to write a paper all in one day, and frequently it is on the day the paper is due. This may seem reasonable for a short paper, but trust me, a good paper is never written in one setting.

There are several stages to writing a good paper, including doing basic research, creating an outline, writing the first draft, editing and revising it, proofreading it, and then reviewing it again. Going through the writing stage is best done over the course of several days, and I suggest you schedule each of the stages to writing your paper for a different day.

I can hear some of you objecting, "But Jim! I can do all of this in a couple of hours!" Sure, I understand, but I also read and grade dozens of papers each week, and I can pick out the papers that were written in one day and those whose author took his/her time and spread it out over the week. One way I can tell is by the quality of thought in the paper.

A WRITING PLAN

Waiting until the last day to write a paper may affect the quality of your paper. It is better to work on a writing assignment over the course of several days. With that in mind, let us look at an example of what this may look like.

On Monday (assuming the paper is due on Sunday at the end of the week), read through the instructions and grading rubric to ensure you understand what is expected in the assignment. This will help you in a couple of ways. First, it will help you budget your time. When you know what is expected, you can plan and schedule the time necessary to complete your assignment. Second, when you read your required reading assignments for the week, you will know what to look for and recognize key points that you will want to reference in your paper. Be sure to take good notes and mark these. It will save you time when you go back to look for these points when writing the draft.

Another reason to do your reading early in the week is it provides you time to reflect on what you have read before you sit down to write a paper. As we discussed in Chapter 9, your mind needs time to ponder and reflect on what you read. If you read the assignment and write your paper on the same day, you rob yourself of the time to reflect on what you read, and in most cases, it shows in the quality of your thought process and critical thinking.

On Tuesday, do some extra research to fill in any gaps or to further explain and clarify your thoughts and ideas. Many classes have optional or suggested textbooks or a list of additional resources to consult each week. Taking advantage of these resources will not only help your understanding of the topic, but it will impress your instructor when he or she sees you referencing these suggested readings.

On Wednesday, draft an outline of your paper. Write the introduction and thesis statement, the main idea for each of your supporting points, and then your conclusion. As you do this, think of your paper as a trail of evidence. Each of your supporting points should lead the reader down the trail toward your conclusion.

This is also the time to include some of the main points you highlighted or noted in your reading assignments. Type in the quotes you want to include for each of your supporting points. At the very least, you should have one quote or idea from your reading and research to back up each supporting point.

On Thursday, write your first draft. When you are done, read it carefully to see if you missed anything and if you addressed all the points in the assignment. Proofreading is key to good writing. While the spelling and grammar check in Microsoft Word is good, it does not catch everything. For instance, you may have used the wrong word in a sentence, but it may still make sense as it is. Therefore, the grammar check may not catch it. Sometimes it is a simple typing error. A good example of this occurred as I wrote this. I mistyped the word "used" as "sued." It was a simple typing error, but grammar check did not catch it because it still made sense. This is why it is important to carefully review your paper to ensure you have used the right words. One way I suggest you proofread your papers is to read it aloud. Your ear will hear mistakes in word usage and grammar that your eye may overlook. I find this tactic most useful and do this with almost everything I write.

This is also when I give it to someone to read and review. This is a very important step, and unfortunately, one that many students overlook. When I ask students about this, I hear responses like, "Well, I don't want anyone to read my paper" or "I am embarrassed because I am not a good writer." I understand these concerns, which is why you need to give it to someone you trust. You will be amazed at how much this helps.

Another reason to ask someone to read your paper is to ensure you did not leave something out. When you do your own research, create an outline, and write a draft, you are familiar with the subject and may not notice that a key point was left out. You may gloss over something because it is all in your head. Someone who is unfamiliar with what you are studying will notice things that do not make sense or sound awkward or incomplete.

When I was in graduate school, I often asked my wife to read over my papers for this very reason. While she is well read and has a working knowledge of many things, she did not know what I had been reading and studying in my class. Therefore, when she read my paper, she could point out areas that did not make sense because she needed more of an explanation. She could also tell me if the information flows (remember: you want to lead them down the path) and if my conclusion made sense. Trust me! This is one of the best things you can do when writing a paper for a grade.

Now it's Friday. Time to write your final draft. Taking into consideration any suggestions made to you from the step above, revise or write your final draft. Once you are done, proofread it for grammatical mistakes, spelling, and writing style.

One of the best resources to help you with this is <u>grammarly. com</u>. You can set up a free account and upload your paper to their website to check for grammar, spelling, and writing style. If you pay for a subscription, you can also download it to your computer as a plugin to Microsoft Word. In addition, as a paid subscriber, you can also check for potential plagiarism.

Now that you have double checked your grammar, spelling, and writing style, complete your final draft. This entire process may take you more than a couple of hours, depending on the length of your paper, so be sure to plan for the time you need.

You are now ready to submit your assignment. If you were able to stick to this suggested schedule, you are all finished, and it is only Friday! Can you see how this would make a difference in the quality of your work versus waiting until Sunday evening to begin?

PLAGIARISM

Before we leave the subject of writing, let's discuss plagiarism, which is a serious matter and one you do not want to mess with. It can lead to failing a class, or even suspension from school.

As part of your proofreading, ensure you have given proper credit to every source you used in your paper. These include quotes and ideas. A misnomer about plagiarism is that you only have to include a citation when you give a direct quote. While this is true, you must also provide a citation to an idea you paraphrased from your sources.

Not understanding how to properly quote and cite your sources is no excuse, either. In most of the cases I run across, avoiding plagiarism is usually a matter of mechanics. If I can see that the student gave credit to the source of their quote, I will make a note of how they should have done it and move on. However, if a paper is comprised of copy and pasted material from one or more websites, and there is no effort to give credit to the source, that is blatant plagiarism and cannot be ignored.

Typically, if plagiarism occurs, a zero is posted for the assignment and a warning given as to the seriousness of plagiarism. It is also reported to the dean or other administrative person at the university, and a note is entered in your records. If it happens a second time in the same class, you may fail the course. You will most likely have a conversation with the academic dean, too. "Three strikes and you're out" applies at most institutions, too. If you are found to have plagiarized a third time, you will most likely be expelled from the institution.

The best way to avoid plagiarism is to know what it is, know how to avoid it, and understand how to cite and reference your sources. A good source to help you with this is www.plagiarism.org. There you will find information about plagiarism, as well as tips on how to avoid it.

Good work takes time. When you take the time to read, reflect, and write, you should see a marked improvement in your papers. Following these simple suggestions has helped me become a better writer and achieve higher grades.

12

UNDERSTANDING THE GRADING FEEDBACK

One of the most valuable things you will get in any education is feedback from your instructor. Good feedback not only shows you what you did right, but it also shows you things you may have missed or done incorrectly, and ways to improve on your next assignment. One of the things I tell my students is I hope my feedback will not only help them understand the grade they earned, but also help them become a better student. So, with that in mind, let's discuss grading comments and feedback.

READ YOUR GRADING COMMENTS

Obviously, you have to read the grading comments to get anything good out of them. Many students do not realize that they receive feedback. They assume the grade is all the feedback they will receive. I run across this situation every now and again. When I explain to a student that if you click on the grade, another window opens with detailed feedback, their entire learning experience changes for the better.

There are two ways you will normally receive feedback, written comments, and a grading rubric. Written comments are made on your paper that highlight things you did well, things you can improve on, or mistakes in writing style, and other comments in general. I use written comments to mark interesting thoughts and ideas as well as to point out where additional information is needed. I also use them to mark incorrect formatting and mistakes in writing style, such as using contractions in academic writing.

The rubric is used to calculate the grade for an assignment. Taking into consideration all my comments and overall impression of the paper, I mark the grading rubric accordingly.

When you receive a grade for an assignment, click on the grade and read through all the comments and grading rubric to see how you did on your paper.

UNDERSTAND THE GRADING COMMENTS

In the feedback, you will typically have a grading rubric listing all the expectations for an assignment along with a mark of where you are in the evaluation. For example, in a written assignment, you may have five different areas graded: Introduction and Conclusion, Thesis, Development and Evidence, Critical Thinking, and Convention and Mechanics. In each of those areas, you might see a mark for Advanced, Proficient, Developing, and Limited. In each area, there is a description of what it takes to achieve a mark in that area. When you get your feedback, you will see how your instructor graded your assignment. You may receive a mark of Advanced in some areas and a mark of Proficient in others, and so on.

Rubric	Advanced	Proficient	Developing
Introduction & Conclusion			
Content Development			
Critical Thinking			
Conventions & Mechanics			

If you have questions or need clarification on any of the marks on the rubric or comments on your paper, contact your instructor. He or she is happy to help you. They want you to succeed in their class, and helping to explain their feedback is one way to do that. I know I always appreciate a student who sends me an email asking for clarification of something I marked on their paper. That shows me that they care about their education and want to make the most of it.

APPLY THE GRADING COMMENTS

One of the most important things you can do to improve your grade in any class is to apply the grading comments to your next assignment. It is also the very essence of why you are there—to learn. Read through your graded assignment and look for ways to correct the mistakes. An instructor notices students who take the time to do this, and not only does it help you improve on every assignment, but it also makes a good impression on you as a student.

Reading, understanding, and applying your grading feedback will not only make you a better student, but you will also learn so much more. I hope you take full advantage of your feedback.

13

A FEW WORDS OF ADVICE

Before we conclude our discussion, let me share with you a few final comments with the hope that they will help you to be a successful online college student.

KEEP TRACK OF YOUR GRADES!

It is important to check assignment grades each week to make sure there are no mistakes. I have had students contact me after the final grades have been posted to point out that there was a mistake with a grade posted three weeks ago. Granted, it was my mistake (I know, hard to believe that instructors make mistakes, but they do!), but the mistake should have been addressed within a few days of the grade being posted.

The reason this is important is an instructor has a deadline to post final grades for a class, usually seven days from the last due date. And once a final grade has been posted, the only way it can be changed is to submit a form to request the change, and there has to be a good reason. A mistake is a good reason, but it would be easier on everyone if the mistake is corrected before final grades are posted.

EXTRA CREDIT

Another question I often get is if a student can do extra credit to help improve their grade. Many schools do not allow extra credit, and I agree. Some students think that extra credit is an easy way to improve their grade, when in fact, it is usually not easy at all. It requires more study and greater depth into the topic.

In my experience, students who ask for extra credit are not doing well in class because they did not complete the required assignments, and now they want an opportunity to make up for it. My first reaction is "if you did not do the required assignments, what makes you think you will do the additional work for extra credit?" Of course, I do not actually say that to a student. Instead, I turn to the policies of the school and follow the guidance outlined in the Student Handbook.

COURSE EXTENSIONS

There are going to be times when something comes up in your life that prevents you from completing a course on time. When this happens, you may have the opportunity to request an extension to submit your assignments. This can be a good thing, but it may cause more challenges than you expect.

For instance, if you request and are approved for an extension for a class, you may get one, two, or even three weeks to complete any outstanding assignments. However, you are probably getting ready to begin a new class, too! So, now you not only have the work to complete for the previous class, but you also have the work to complete in the class that just started. This is something to consider.

Course extensions are not automatic. Most schools have specific criteria that must be met. For instance, a student must be passing the course when the situation that prevented them from completing their work came up. In other words, procrastinating and falling behind are not valid reasons to request an extension.

There are several reasons a request for an extension may be warranted. Things such as military deployment, unexpected business trips, illness, or injuries are a few reasons an extension is approved. Just keep in mind that you may have to provide documentation, too.

You may be surprised to learn that technical difficulties is not a reason to approve an extension. I often have students ask for an extension because their computer crashed, or their Internet was shut off. As unfortunate as these types of things are, there is normally a work-around, such as going to the library to submit your assignments, or a coffee shop to access the Internet. Free Internet is everywhere; you just have to look for it.

The best thing to do if you think you may need an extension is to contact your instructor as soon as you can to find out your options. In most cases, they will work with you and with a little extra work, you should be able to complete the course on time.

14

FINAL THOUGHTS

Congratulations! You now have a good idea of what it takes to succeed in an online class.

In the first section, we learned about some of the things you need to do to be prepared for your first class. You need a computer and a good, reliable Internet connection. There are also a few apps you should have, along with a basic understanding of how to use them. You need your textbooks on the first day of class. You also learned the value of conducting an orientation of your virtual campus and classroom. With all these resources, you are equipped to begin your educational journey.

After reading the second section, you learned how to communicate with your instructor and classmates. You also learned some of the basics to effective communication and how this will benefit you in both your education and profession. Perhaps most importantly, you have a plan to budget and manage your time so you keep up with everything in class. We also discussed the importance of taking responsibility for your education. Now you have some of the foundational skills you need to manage your education.

Then, in the third section, you learned a few strategies to achieve success in online learning. You have a strategy to complete your reading assignments, participate in online discussions, and write papers. You also learned the importance of reviewing, understanding, and applying the feedback your instructor provides.

We then discussed a few other things that may come up in your education, things like extra credit and course extensions, which are available, if needed, but should be avoided, if possible.

All in all, you have a good foundation to begin your educational journey, manage yourself and your classes, and a few strategies to succeed in online classes and ultimately graduate with a college degree.

If I can leave you with one more piece of advice, it would be this: Stay on top of things! It is very easy to fall into the trap of procrastination, thinking, "I can always do it tomorrow." Before you know it, tomorrow is here, and now you have to catch up.

Make a commitment to yourself to make the most of this book and develop good habits in your educational journey. Plan your time and work your plan. If you do, you will be a successful online college student.

Online education is a great way to get to where you want to be. Through education, you truly can transform your life! —Jim

ACKNOWLEDGMENTS

This book is the culmination of many years working with students, teaching students, and, of course, being a student. There are several people I would like to thank who have helped to inspire me in ways they may not even realize.

First, Dr. Debra Hudson. Debra took me to lunch one day when I was working for Colorado Christian University in Grand Junction and suggested I consider teaching a new course designed for new and incoming students. She said my experience as a graduate of CCU, a member of the staff at CCU, and now a graduate student would give me a unique perspective to share with our students. If it were not for her suggestion, I may not be teaching today.

Dr. Kristen Wall. She was the Director of Faculty Development for many of my years at CCU and is the one who first mentioned the term Professional Adjunct to me. Prior to that, I had not heard the term, but I immediately grabbed on to it, which eventually led to this book and my working with students online.

Mike Moroney. Mike believed in me and gave me the opportunity to do more than I thought I could do. He chose me to fill in as an interim director in Grand Junction, and then offered me the chance to open and run my own center. He was my role model and mentor during that time. Thanks, Mike!

To Dave, Charles, Bill, and many others who were my undergraduate instructors, and later, my colleagues at CCU. As my instructors, you inspired me in more ways than I can list. When I began teaching, you were the ones I turned to for advice and suggestions.

To my many friends, co-workers, and colleagues at CCU. I think back on the joy of working with Linda, Darris, Margena, Joelle, Lisa, Josh, Linda, Rob, and especially Vickie, who helped keep me organized and always had a smile. I have fond memories of working alongside all of you and count myself as truly blessed to know you.

The same goes for everyone at Moody Bible Institute and Colorado Technical University. Although we worked in a virtual working environment, you all inspired me to take my teaching to the next level.

And most of all, I want to thank my best friend, partner, and wife, Beth. You have always been at my side, encouraging me (pushing me sometimes!) to continue as a student, administrator, and now educator. I could not have done this without your love and support. I love you!

And, of course, my students. You are the reason I do what I do.

ABOUT THE AUTHOR

Before committing to teaching full time, Jim was a member of the staff at Colorado Christian University. At CCU, he had several responsibilities, including enrollment counseling, academic advising, and directing a center for adult and graduate studies. All in all, he has worked with students from application to graduation.

Jim began his educational journey at the age of 18, attending Iowa State University. As he would tell you, he had a great time, but did not do so well in school because he had no idea what he wanted to do. After dropping out of ISU, Jim enlisted in the Army. About three years into his new career, he decided to take college courses. This was before online education, so each time he was transferred to a new Army base, he had to transfer colleges, too. All in all, he attended four colleges and universities during his military career. When he retired, he transferred all his credits—about three years' worth—to one university, then another, and then another, before finally finding a school that worked for him. Being an adult with a family and work obligations, he needed flexibility, which led him to non-traditional education. In 2003, at the age of 41, Jim graduated from Colorado Christian University with a degree in Organizational Management.

A few years later, Jim began taking courses at Denver Seminary, but after one year, took a leave of absence to complete a Master of

Science degree in Education from Capella University. Jim completed all the coursework at Capella online. After that, he returned to Denver Seminary to continue his studies. Again, as before, he found it difficult to take courses offered on campus and work full time. The commute to the seminary was 90 minutes each way. He stuck with it long enough to complete a Graduate Certificate in Theology, and then transferred to Knox Theological Seminary, where he continued his studies online and completed a Master of Arts in Biblical and Theological Studies.

Prior to his career in education, Jim retired with honors from the United States Army in 1998. His tours of duty took him across the United States and overseas to Korea, Germany, and the Middle East.

Jim and his wife, Beth, have been married for over 35 years and live in Greeley, Colorado. They have three adult children. Their daughter lives on the east coast with her husband. Their oldest son recently graduated from Colorado School of Mines with a degree in Environmental Engineering. And their youngest son is studying at the University of Northern Colorado.

When Jim is not busy teaching, writing, or creating tutorials for his website, you will find him on the golf course or with his wife, enjoying the mountains of Colorado.

RESOURCES

Enhance your success in online education and join the community at Online College Success ™ where we offer several ways to help you on your educational journey.

GO TO THE ONLINE COLLEGE SUCCESS ™ SITE AT www.OnlineCollegeSuccess.com to:

- Sign up for the free newsletter with tips and resources

- Follow the Life as a Student Blog

- Learn about upcoming tutorials and online courses

- Schedule an appearance by the author

FOLLOW US ON SOCIAL MEDIA

- Like us on Facebook at https://www.facebook.com/onlinecollegesuccess/

- Follow us on Twitter at https://twitter.com/onlineedsuccess/

PERSONAL COACHING AND MENTORING

Jim is available to be your personal academic coach to help you get started, learn how to manage your time, and develop good habits that every student needs. If you want to discuss coaching and mentoring opportunities with Jim, go to https://OnlineCollegeSuccess. com/contact-us/ and click on the link to complete a brief survey of your interests and needs.

ONLINE COLLEGE SUCCESS TUTORIALS AND ONLINE COURSES

We offer several self-paced tutorials on APA and MLA styles, plagiarism, and other writing tools. In addition, we have online courses in academic writing that go more in depth and teach you how to be an effective writer in an education setting.